EMPATH AND SELF INTROSPECTION

The Science of Highly Sensitive People – Master
Your Personality, Overcome Fears and Nurture
Your Gift

AHLIA ROSE

losses, direct or indirect, which are incurred as a result of the use of information contained within this document, including, but not limited to, errors, omissions, or inaccuracies.

Table of Contents

INTRODUCTION

Ahlia Rose takes you by the hand as an experienced empath and intuitive coach; her book, written from an empath's perspective, explores and encourages you to note the red flags, grow from your experiences, and embrace your intuition.

If you struggle with overwhelming feelings, loneliness, or feel like you don't belong in the world, you will find this book remedial.

This book is perfect for empaths trying to understand who they truly are while trying to cope in the world.

Follow Your North Node

"There's nowhere you can be, that isn't were you are meant to be" _____

John Lennon

CHAPTER ONE: CHARACTERISTICS OF AN EMPATH

If you know you are an empath, you probably are already aware of the many characteristics that go with the term. However, for those wanting to discover more about being a highly sensitive being, see how many things are relatable to you. Here are most of the characteristics of an empath and the pros and cons that go with them. Let's dive in!

Highly Tuned Senses

I always thought I had a good sense of smell and hearing, but how do you know? Well, for empaths, it usually becomes apparent when you notice things way before others because of your heightened senses. It helps make us empaths feel more intensely, which is a pro, in my opinion. We can experience things more vividly; however, this can sometimes also work against us in times of chaos or loud, disruptive noises.

Love of Nature

Empaths love nature and surrounding themselves in a natural environment. It provides us with peace from the chaotic world and is a way for us to recharge our energy levels. After spending time alone in a park or by the beach, most empaths feel rejuvenated. Personally, this is my favorite way to re-align myself when I feel emotionally exhausted. It will also mean you have enormous respect for your environment and the planet as you connect to it emotionally. You feel amazed looking at beautiful old trees rooted in the earth. It just pulls on your heartstrings. So, for that matter, you will want to protect your surroundings by being passionate about saving the planet.

When you see an earthly injustice such as polluting or damage to the earth, it hurts you deeply. Relating to nature as your energy source, you may also become depressed in the winter when the days are shorter. It is known as Seasonal Affective Disorder, which is, funnily enough, abbreviated as SAD. Empaths are also affected by the moon and planetary elements, as they reflect their energies onto the earth. Therefore, it might also be a good idea to learn astrology basics, which we will do in one of the chapters.

Pick up on Energy and Emotions of Others

It is the key to being an empath. Sure, many people can be saddened by others in troubled times, but this is different from feeling a wave of intense emotion overcome you. For example, if someone is sad and distraught, then an empath will recognize that within a person, even if that same person isn't crying or showing their emotions. Energetically, for some unexplained reason, we can feel or sense the feeling of other individuals, especially if they are loved ones or people we cherish. Each of us can feel at different levels. Some may have stronger emotions, feelings, or instincts.

The pros of this are that it makes empaths unique, as they can provide healing energy to others on earth and understand emotions like no one else. It comes to a downfall; sometimes, we cannot clearly distinguish our feelings from others, leaving empaths feeling confused and overwhelmed in life.

Highly Intuitive

One of my most loved gifts is my intuition. Empaths will have the ability to recognize their intuition. It is that deep, subtle inner knowing that regularly talks to an empath, guiding them along the way. It is a developed gift over time, but most empaths will find they already have a powerful intuition at a young age. For this reason, we generally know when people are lying or hiding something through our intuition. It may be challenging to put things into words, which can sometimes be frustrating for an empath.

You're a Good Listener

People will often compliment you on your listening skills. However, it is not just your skills as a listener; it is because you have a deeper understanding of emotions. It is since you generally get what the other person may be experiencing. As you are more in touch with your feelings, you will better recognize them and relate to them in others. It can feel rewarding helping others or feeling connected to another human emotionally.

But unfortunately, most empaths find it difficult not to jeopardize themselves while giving help. Many people can take advantage of an empath's good nature, leaving them with emotional baggage and feelings of neglect.

Battle with Boundaries

As a child and teenager, I never understood what boundaries were. I came from an Italian family, so that didn't help, lol. Empaths struggle with boundaries, and I don't know an empath who cannot somehow relate. Having the ability to feel and want to fix the world's issues, we battle with feeling like we must help others, generally at the risk of ourselves. Most of us must work hard to understand our energy and learn how to say no, as we are worried about hurting others or feeling guilty for not helping. We prioritize the emotions of others over our own and shield out our deeper feelings.

These suppressed emotions and lack of attention to ourselves often add to an empath's sense of low self-esteem.

People Tell You Their Problems

I am not talking about one occasion where the lady at the grocery store tells you her whole life story. It is something that can happen quite often. When you meet new people for the first time, they will energetically be drawn to you and your energy. They sense your soft nature and find it comforting to talk to you because they feel wise to understand them. Therefore, you probably find it easy to meet people and hold a conversation. People love being around your energy, but be mindful as they can drain your positive, upbeat nature and burden you with their life stories, as they don't understand your gift.

You See the World Differently

Another thing I love about being an empath is that you experience your way around, seeing things that people regularly miss. You may be aware of your physical surroundings, noticing a bird singing while hearing other sounds.

Seeing the beauty in the world is a lovely gift, as your senses most likely will be heightened, you will slow down with the world to admire it.

A great way to keep positive is to notice these things, which comes naturally for an empath.

Craving Solitude

Empaths need to spend time alone to process their feelings. As we are absorbing so much, having time alone is a way of refilling up our cup. Solitude is something an empath is comfortable with and will enjoy. Too much time alone, however, may lead to overthinking and a disconnect with others.

Therefore, empaths need to be social with at least one other person who understands and respects them, offering sound advice and support.

You Find it Hard to Cope with Sensory Overload

Empaths shy away from loud and excessive noise, crowds, or chaotic situations. With highly acute senses, an overload will leave empaths feeling confused and sometimes disorientated, a condition most of us like to avoid.

Struggle with Vulnerability & Intimacy

A characteristic most empaths are shy to admit we feel emotionally exposed as we struggle with feeling vulnerable in the world. In intimate situations, sometimes we feel too much or have a fear of getting hurt, so much that it is often easier for us to shut that part of ourselves off. That is why empaths can have a difficult time in relationships and getting close to others.

You Lead with Your Heart

Your emotions are your guide, so you tend to dive into situations with your heart first. Not always the best action applied, but for an empath, this is who we are, and we generally don't trust or know any other way. On a positive note, when you make a decision led with your heart, it comes from your most authentic self, which can be rewarding. On the other hand, throwing yourself heart first without thinking things over can lead to heartache. There needs to be a balance.

Children and Animals are Attracted to You

Both children and animals have a better sense of self, and they are also less prone to having too many worries, which makes them more open to using their senses. Like us, they can easily detect the energy of others. As empaths tend to have **caring nature,** kids and animals can pick up on this, which is why they are drawn to us. Sometimes I also find interesting characters drawn to me as well, for the same reasons. The benefits of having animals and children drawn to you are that they also have high vibe energy, which makes an empath feel recharged and happy.

Desire to Feel Understood

Empath's biggest desire is to feel understood. As we tend to understand most others, it is challenging for an empath to feel the same. When we feel connected with another human being who may be similar or have the same vibrancy and compassion, we are delighted. The experience can leave an amplified feeling of joy and a sense of placement with other like-minded souls. Empaths suffer a lot; they feel alone as no one feels the world quite like them. But take comfort in knowing there are other empaths out there who have similar experiences to you.

Feel Physically & Mentally Tired

Using your energy daily to stay positive and help heal the world can leave you feeling exhausted. When you feel so many emotions, whether it be yours or others, it tends to leave you feeling overwhelmed and drained. It explains why many empaths struggle with feeling tired all the time. The importance of time alone and recharging your energy to maintain a balance is vital for an empath. Although it is normal to feel tired, I found that it was not suitable to be a continuous cycle. When I was healing from something, there was a valid reason for the zapped energy levels. You need to understand why you feel tired and apply positive action before it becomes a habit and leads to other on-going symptoms.

Need to Feel Wanted, Valued & Loved

Empaths can be complicated creatures to understand, but we ultimately want to be loved like everyone else. We might experience physical or emotional abuse, neglect, bullying, or something similar. Therefore, our need to feel valued or wanted by others is intensified.

Most empaths also hate to feel like a burden on others, making it difficult for them to accept support from people. It makes it tricky in relationships as people can have a hard time trying to understand our needs. Empaths can feel **overwhelmed in relationships** and struggle to attract the right people due to their lack of self-worth.

You are Honest

Most empaths are honest or will find an alternative way of telling the truth if they don't want to hurt others' feelings. Honesty is a rare characteristic these days, which is respected and appreciated among many. Sometimes an empath may struggle to find the right words to express their truth as they overthink how it will affect the other person, rather than be straightforward.

Ability to Predict Things

I feel this is god's way of giving an empath the gift of guidance and sharing his knowledge with us. Each empath will be uniquely talented with predictions, but if they have learned to develop their intuition, their ability to predict things will be more powerful. It is a beautiful gift of an empath that should be nurtured. Like myself, some empaths may struggle with this talent leaving them to feel isolated, confused, or alone. Such abilities can come in the form of signs, dreams, synchronicities, predictions of the past, or future involving loved ones or events.

Low Self-Esteem or Worth

Today, I still struggle with this one; building confidence is critical for an empath. Learning to trust yourself and your capabilities can transform your life, particularly for an empath. As most of us have experienced our fair share of toxic relationships or past traumas, we have had to address our feelings first hand.

Forgetting our inner guidance can mean you become clouded with self-doubting thoughts. If you have false beliefs from life experience, abusive behavior, negativity, or being judged, it can stop you from developing your sense of worth. Often an empath will have re-occurring thoughts and emotions triggered by others about themselves. It is just a sign that these emotions may require addressing.

You Dislike Conflict

Run, run as fast as you can. All empaths dislike conflict and try to avoid it at all costs. But if you tend to find yourself in a situation where someone has hurt you badly, they may experience another side of the empath. Remember that addressing conflict is a healthy part of any relationship. Talking and expressing your point of view is just as important as listening to another. And this is linked back to being assertive and emotionally in tune with your needs.

You Easily Get Bored

Some people say that **empaths develop addictions**, it may be true in some cases, but I think it is a personal experience for each of us. Nevertheless, you may find yourself bored easily, as you are accustomed to being highly stimulated all the time. Be it through emotion, nature, or just a desire to live life to its fullest by experiencing joy. Learn to be okay with being bored; find interesting ways to express your creative energy.

Introverted

It is no secret; empaths are introverts. Empaths need time to contemplate and think about life, process our thoughts and feelings as we are more open to exploring and questioning ourselves. We thrive during important and meaningful discussions about life, as we feel understood. Small talk can be shallow and tedious as there is hardly any emotion or juice in the topic.

You Feel Like You Don't Fit in

Emotionally confused, too sensitive, unstable, free-spirited; these are all things that empaths may have been referred to by other people. Often, I have felt like I was from another planet and so different from everyone else. I felt so alone like no one understood what was in my heart and the intensity of how I felt things. There were times when I tried to block my gifts and reject them, but that just backfired. I learned that the desire to want to fit in was only a natural human condition. Once I distinguished my need for why I behaved like this, I let go and embraced who I was.

Open to Exploring the Non-Physical

Having non-physical gifts and talents can be intimidating and exciting at the same time. Each time I received an intuitive message, from my guides, spirit, or whatever you believe in, it gave me an adrenalin rush. It was like a confirmation that I was not alone and was on the right path.

As an empath, you have a strong **sense of finding your purpose** and using your gifts to help others. Because you experience energetical connections, it makes you more open to exploring the non-physical and your spirituality.

There are also many other characteristics related to being an empath, and these can include;

- Being a creative person
- Feel a pull towards holistic or healing therapy
- Always fatigued
- Like to back the underdog
- Suffer from lower back problems or digestive disorders
- Watching violence, tragedy on TV can be unbearable
- You can have an addictive personality
- Strive for the truth
- Appear shy or moody
- Finds routine or rules restricting
- Likes to daydream

Writing Task

Take a journal or notebook and write down any of the characteristics you have as an empath. Some of them might be different from the ones in this book. Each chapter, we will work little by little, helping you to understand yourself better, leading you to create healthier habits and routines to build on.

Follow Your North Node

"All I ever wanted was to reach out and touch another human being not just with my hands but with my heart" _____

Tahereh Mafi

CHAPTER TWO: TYPES OF EMPATHS & GIFTS

UNDERSTANDING YOURSELF

In life, it is essential to have a sense of identity and to understand where your emotions, beliefs, and thoughts all stem from. The more we can put ourselves in question, the better humans we become, the more our souls evolve. Taking responsibility for our own emotions and actions means that we can grow from past mistakes. Dedicating time to understand yourself will help you gain clarity as to why you behave in specific ways. We all have reasons for doing things the way we do. Whether we realize it or not, to us, it is just a normal part of our being. When we address these so-called 'normality's' and try to understand them from an outsider point of view, then we can begin to put ourselves in question. You may ask yourself why you act a certain way in a relationship, rather than excuse it as a personality trait. Maybe you are carrying beliefs from past experiences that hold you back into your future.

EXPLORING YOUR WORTH

How do you view yourself? Do you see yourself as fragile or trapped in a chaotic world, or are you a sensitive soul who challenges society's norms? Empaths typically struggle with a lack of worth, and it is mainly because of their high sensitivity and past experiences. We forget how to trust ourselves and our judgment and quickly become clouded by other people or what is happening globally. The first step to becoming a confident empath is understanding you have a gift and treat it with honor and respect.

TYPES OF EMPATHS

Okay, so you may know you're an empath because of the ability you have to channel other's emotions, but how well do you know your gifts? You will find that people will say that there are empathetic towards others. However, it goes beyond the simple act of putting yourself in someone else's shoes. For an empath, you will easily become overwhelmed with emotions that you have tuned into from your surroundings; it's a daily grind which often can leave you feeling exhausted with life.

Nevertheless, some beautiful things go with being an empath. These can relate to feeling like you have a special non-physical connection with spirit and experiencing your surroundings with your senses more intensely. So, being an empath isn't a terrible thing, once you learn to shield yourself and gift in a way where you are entirely respecting yourself.

Here are briefly some of the types of empaths. You may find you can relate to many of these or fit into more than one.

Physical empaths can feel the physical pain of another person.

Emotional empaths feel the emotions of a person. It is generally what most empaths will identify.

Intuitive empaths have strong inner knowing and gut feelings; intuition is a gift of many empaths.

Plant empaths are those in tune with the needs of plants, it may come naturally to you, and you may feel that being surrounded by plants makes you feel completely content.

Animal empaths are passionate about animals and can naturally feel the needs of them. They usually end up working with animals as vets or could become an advocate for them.

Heyoka empaths are known as the most powerful empaths. Often, they have psychic abilities, known for being born breached and commonly provide a way for others to help them overcome feelings of weakness. In native America, ' Heyoka' refers to clown; this type of empath will also use humor to challenge people. Heyoka's have a way of knowing the right thing to say and ask people the questions that make them think about their own lives. For this reason, many may come to you for advice. You help reflect who people indeed are to them, maybe without knowing. Heyoka's tend to look younger than their age and generally will never admit they are one.

Earth empaths have a deep connection to the planet. They can often predict when something may happen, such as a natural disaster. Earth empaths can also tune into our solar system and the planets.

Dream empaths can have dreams or visions of the future, past, or loved ones. They are also considered as precognitive empaths. These dreams are often strong feelings associated with them that sticks with the empath in a way only they can interpret.

SOME SCIENCE EXPLAINED SIMPLY

Did you know that introverted empaths have *increased sensitivity to dopamine*? Dopamine is a natural chemical in the brain that makes us feel good. It is a chemical that is responsible for transmitting signals between the nerve cells and the brain. By having increased sensitivity, this means that we need less dopamine to feel happy.

Having a higher sensitivity also makes us more connected with the planet and its electromagnetic fields. Humans are made of energy, tiny electrical currents; *both the heart and brain generate electromagnetic fields;* they provide information about other emotions and thoughts. These fields are on the earth and our sun, it could explain why empaths feel affected by the weather and their surroundings more than most others.

Research has found that there is a particular brain cell that is responsible for compassion.

Can you imagine the size of an empaths compassionate cell? It works by acting as a mirror for us to share in another person's emotion, triggered by outside events from ourselves so you can experience what another person does. It is known as the *Mirror Neuron System.*

Emotional Contagion is when individuals feel or express emotions similar to others. In other words, you don't just observe the feelings of others, but they affect your emotional state.

The most important function of this is, it makes social interaction smoother, as it forms an emotional closeness between people. Isn't it always better when you feel someone understands your feelings? Sometimes we tend to copy other body languages without even realizing it.

The term *Mirror-touch Synesthesia* is a rare condition where individuals experience a similar sensation in the same or opposite part of the body as another.

Watching someone stroke someone's hair and being able to feel the same sense yourself. The stimulus causes a person to experience the sensation. Mirror-touch Synesthesia exists in around 1.6 to 2.5% of the population.

Synesthesia is a neurological condition when two different senses are paired in the brain. It makes a person experience cross response to stimuli like taste or sound. For example, when you hear a piece of music, you see color.

EMPATH'S GIFTS

As for us, Empaths are born with these unique gifts, and it is also our responsibility to protect how we share them. Some of the advantages you may find you possess could be that you have *natural healing energy*. You magically soothe people, and they feel connected with you because you understand their deepest desires.

Empaths also have the gift of *heightened senses*. Empaths are very *intuitive* with the ability to be,

Clairvoyant – Meaning where you can see things through the mind's third eye.

Clairaudient – Meaning where you can hear things in your mind's voice.

Clairsentient – Meaning where you can smell things that don't have a physical source.

Clair knowing – Meaning where you can sense things.

Clairgustance – Meaning where you can taste things that are not there.

It may be that you'll generally be able to sniff something out way before others can, which could be highly beneficial in certain situations of danger.

Being an empath can mean you can sense, feel, or be in tune with your environment and those around you in a vibrational way. It makes you *emotionally intelligent* because you can identify with feelings faster and understand the triggers that come with them. It's like the universe talks to you through your heightened senses and the emotions you feel. It can often mean you also possess gifts of being Telepathic or a medium because you are most likely open to the non-physical, sensing things on an energetic level. Sometimes this can be about a person's past or future, making you a valuable guide to helping others reflect on aspects of their lives. Thus, meaning you are an extremely treasured friend while assisting in the healing of people. Empaths can often feel like guardian angels on earth, helping to heal and uplift the planet, that is why you may also discover you resonate with being a lightworker.

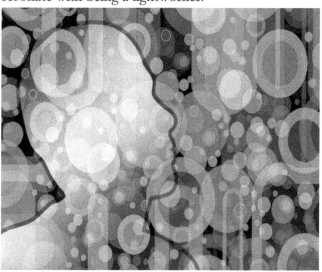

DEVELOPING YOUR EMPATH GIFTS

Understanding your gift is vital for an empath, so you can use it in ways where you can help others without jeopardizing yourself in the process.

You may have noticed during your childhood that you felt different from other people. Mainly because of the sensitivity you felt in situations beyond your control as a child. Most empaths generally realize there is something special about them; it's like an inner knowing. I recall when I was around ten years old, my family and I went on vacation. While driving home along the windy road, I felt a presence telling me something would happen, but not to be afraid. It wasn't that I saw someone telling me this. It was instead a powerful energetic download of information that came through via my guardian or guide. Feeling anxious, I kept telling my dad to be mindful around each corner as I held tight to my baby sister, who was also in the backseat sitting next to me. I wanted the feeling to go away, it was so uncomfortable, and I felt like I was becoming paranoid. Lone behold, our car lost control, swerving onto the other side of the road. It all happened so quickly; it was like a flash before our eyes.

I felt the car spin, and at the same time, I could feel an incredible force holding me down. Even today, as I write about it, recalling the event, I can feel the adrenaline run through my body. We Landed into a ditch off the main road just centimeters from smashing into a large tree. Shaken up, I saw the look of horror on my parent's face checking over their shoulder at us in the back seat. We walked away from the situation without a scratch. I recall wiping the tears from my face as the fear of it all was relived in my mind. The thing that frightened me most was that I knew it would happen, because I felt it, which I struggled to understand. It was hard to know why as I had no idea what empaths were. Being in the late 1980s, people didn't start using the internet until 1991.

Of course, you all probably have stories of your own, but this was one of the many messages that came to me through my intuition when I was young.

Let's look at some of the gifts mentioned above and how you can learn to develop them better.

Natural healers can improve their abilities by trusting themselves more and learning to let go of the fear-based around being used or drained by others. Understand that you can heal yourself just the way you heal others. It is only that most of us tend to focus on others so much we sometimes forget this. Learning from past mistakes is very important for an empath. If someone treats you in a way where you do not feel respected, ask yourself what you can do differently next time to protect your energy.

Your *heightened senses* can increase when we make time for ourselves and focus on enjoying the things around us that we can hear, smell, touch, taste, and see. Being grateful for our senses and gifts also helps to nurture these. It is like telling the universe how much you appreciate your gifts, and in turn, it continues to provide more.

Developing your intuition is an integral part of being an empath. Sometimes along the way, after turbulent encounters in relationships, an empath can lose faith in their abilities to trust their judgment. It has happened to me various times when I have felt manipulated or taken for granted by others. The important thing to remember here is that we are human, like everyone else.

I realized that because empaths feel more, it can also lead to feeling more disappointed with ourselves. Our high expectations we may place on ourselves to use our gift with others can sometimes overshadow the need for necessary boundaries. Learning to trust yourself and your intuition is vital. I build my intuition by asking for answers from within and listening to any emotions, feelings, or signs that come up. I also like to seek guidance with my spirit guides, who I communicate with internally. My favorite way is to use oracle or tarot cards when I need instant clarification on something that keeps me stuck. Learning to read tarot cards was a process that became much easier than I thought. I watched various readers on YouTube to understand what most of the cards meant, but I soon discovered that I understood the story through the energy I felt. For me, this was a great way to build my gifts, so if you have not already, I would suggest experimenting with some oracle cards to start with, then move onto tarot if you feel it works for you.

Another way to build on your intuition is to acknowledge when you knew something would play out in a certain way. It will help you to strengthen your confidence in yourself and appreciate your gift.

Being *emotionally intelligent* is a natural gift for empaths; however, our feelings can sometimes get overly cluttered when we forget to discharge and clear out our energies. Being clear in your emotions means you can pick up on things better and tell the difference between your feelings and those around you. Making a routine to disconnect and ground yourself should be practiced regularly, as it is how most of us recharge our battery.

Some of the best ways to enhance and look after your gifts naturally come with spending time in solitude. Luckily most of us crave this. If you do not already, then you should practice meditation in your daily routine. Not only will it help you to feel calm and in control, but after some time, it will be a pleasurable way of escaping from the realities of the world around you. I understand meditation is not for everyone. Before I succeeded, I failed many times. When I went through my awakening, I became so dedicated and focused because I truly desired to have a different feeling of relief. When the time is right for you, meditation can work wonders. In the meantime, if you struggle after repetitive attempts, try other methods of relaxation. They could be in the form of being creative through art, writing, planting, cooking, etc.

By spending time exploring your thoughts and feelings, you will not only become wiser, but you'll also develop more patience for yourself.

Writing Task

What kind of empath do you think you are? What are some of your gifts? Feel free to write about an experience you had recently or as a child, expressing yourself on paper. Feel the emotions that come and go. How can you better learn to embrace your gifts in the future?

Follow Your North Node

"Love and Compassion are the true religions to me. But to develop this, we do not need to believe in any religion" _____

Dali Lama XIV

CHAPTER THREE:
CHALLENGES AS AN EMPATH

EMPATH WARNING SIGNS

Most of the time, empaths indeed realize they need time to recharge, it is already too late. One of the challenges we face is burning ourselves out. Like most others, we have a level of tolerance we need to acknowledge. Understanding that no one benefits when you burn out or allow yourself to become milked emotionally will help to make you feel less guilty.

The power is always yours, especially when you feel like you have lost control of a situation or your sense of identity. Come back to yourself, your core, and inner knowing. Take time out when you feel overwhelmed or exhausted and learn to make yourself a priority. God put you on this planet to look after yourself and your gift so you can share it with others, not so you can let yourself be abused or mistreated. Learn the warning signs that come with needing time out.

If you feel any of these things on occasion, it is only familiar, as they generally come with being an empath. Learn to distinguish the warning signs when you need to hold back and refill your cup.

Sleeping is a significant way for our bodies to recharge and our cells to renew. When we go through shifts and energetic upgrades, we feel the need to sleep more, so honor and listen to your body. Sometimes when we are healing, we may require more sleep or want to curl up in a ball and hide in our pain.

Just know that this period will pass and be extra mindful of the amount of time you spend in bed. Balance it out with some regular exercise. When I went through a break up from a narcissistic relationship, I longed for the time when I went to sleep. Mainly because it was a quiet time when my emotions would come to the surface, I would often find I'd cry myself to sleep, as it was my way of admitting to my truths. Showing myself compassion, I allowed all my suppressed emotions to come out. Over time I realized that I no longer needed to cry anymore. I knew then that it was time for me to shake up my energy as I started to feel like I wanted to move on from this nightmare. I promised that I would allow my emotions to express themselves more clearly rather than brush them aside next time.

Mental health issues like anxiety or depression can be common in an empath's experience. It is why we need to address our feelings and treat them as valuable as we treat those around us. While I was in my narcissistic relationship, I fell into a depression state as I denied my feelings telling me to get out of this toxic relationship. The guy I was dating had a terrible childhood where he saw his own parents battle abuse.

As an empath, I felt very sorry for him having to have gone through such a challenging childhood. But in turn, what I failed to ignore was that he was reflecting that same kind of abuse onto me. There is no excuse for anyone to treat you this way, whether it was done to them or not. It is our responsibility to learn, grow from our life lessons.

Understanding the warning signs of anxiety or depression can mean that you can shift your awareness onto the solution. Admitting there is something wrong is the first step to helping yourself.

My depression came to the forefront when a few friends of mine brought up their concern as they saw patterns in my eating behavior. I had completely lost my appetite, and once I ordered food, I found that I could only stomach a couple of spoons. It was because of the turning feeling I always had in the pit of my stomach. I was miserable and felt worthless. My partner had often spoken to me in a way that put me down and made me feel like I was not good enough for him. At first glance, I was offended by my friend's remarks and was in complete denial. Then I was forced to look at myself and soon realized I needed to find a way out.

Depression and anxiety can come from many different triggers, not just in a relationship. It can relate to a lack of purpose, feeling out of control with your surroundings, or even triggers from past childhood events. Be open to accepting help from others, particularly those around you who love and care for you. I never told anyone what was happening to me in my relationship and the issues I was facing each day. I felt ashamed and guilty. Understanding the warning signs of anxiety or depression can mean that you can shift your awareness onto the solution. Admitting there is something wrong is the first step to helping yourself.

Some of the signs of **depression** could relate to;

- Constantly feeling down
- Becoming withdrawn from friends or family members
- Changes in appetite, weight loss, or gain
- Crying for no reason
- Feelings of worthlessness
- Changes in sleeping patterns
- Restlessness
- Diminished sex drive
- Headaches

Remember that depression is often a symptom of something bigger that needs to be addressed. It is not a part of who you are, rather emotions that need to surface. Talking to someone can often make you feel better. However, if you find yourself in a state for a long period consulting a professional could provide you with techniques to help. These days it is a familiar feeling to experience, so there is no need to feel embarrassed or have too much pride to admit. Doing so will only make you wiser and emotionally intelligent in distinguishing it and helping others who feel the same way.

Anxiousness and depression can often go hand in hand. It can make you feel like the situation is much worse than it is. Sometimes simple acts like taking public transport or being in large crowds can trigger anxiety.

I remember suffering from mild anxiety at different periods in my life. They mainly had to do with going out after I broke up from my toxic relationship. All I wanted to do was hide away from everyone in the world. I knew I was wounded, vulnerable, and didn't want to expose myself to anyone else who may take advantage of my current state. In a way, I was lucky, as I understood why I was feeling anxious, so it felt like I had more control over it. Finding ways to help soothe me, I managed to overcome it. I often allowed myself to balance spending time alone and one on one with friends until I felt more ready to tackle small groups of friends.

The most important thing to remember is that if you find it is controlling your life, you should seek someone who understands anxiousness and how to cope better with the symptoms. I know loved ones who battled anxiety when they lost a parent or went through challenging times. Sometimes it is because we are trying to process difficult or overwhelming emotions in an intense period.

Some of the common symptoms of **anxiety** are

- Trembling or sweaty hands
- Lack of ability to concentrate or perform ordinary tasks
- Shortness of breath
- Increased heart rate
- Sweating or hot or cold flushes
- Edgy
- Dizziness
- Stomach or chest pain
- Feeling weak or tired
- Difficulty sleeping or nightmares

If any of these symptoms impact your life, seeking assistance through a counselor or medical professional can help support you.

Some of the other warning signs that show you need to address emotions could be repeating cycles in relationships, feeling fatigued constantly, or noticing physical health problems such as back pain. These could mean you need some time out for yourself or that you need to address some issues on a deeper level.

Acknowledge any addictive behaviors like drinking alcohol, eating food, having sex, or impulse buying, to feel better. These are all quick fixes to try and temporarily hide emotions or give us a rush. Shopping was once the way I gave myself an adrenalin rush. But the thing was that it never lasted long enough, so it was a cycle that kept repeating its self.

Material items only give you a certain amount of gratification, if you haven't noticed. Rather than seeking aid in the act of buying or doing something, try understanding your emotions, why you feel the need for these things. For me, it became a temporary relief to looking and feeling better by having new clothes. I was also passionate about fashion and design, so it was a way of expressing myself. Therefore, I found another way to express my feelings through cooking or writing while looking at this addiction. Saving for long term bigger goals meant that I could put the money spent aside and plan things like a vacation.

GIVING YOUR POWER AWAY

Unfortunately, it is often too easy for us to give our power away. It comes with the territory of being an open energy field exposed to the world's vibrations. Over time you will learn it doesn't have to be that way. Some empaths may not like what I am about to say, but it is true, giving your power away is an option. I have learned the hard way, and I am guessing you will probably too.

It doesn't matter if it is a loving partner or parent. You have the strength and power within you to know when to step back and hold tight for yourself. Of course, it is okay for you to be there for the other person. However, you need to realize when it is troubling you too much and when to step away.

When my mother lost her father, she went through various things that were not there initially. Subtle signs of anxiety and grief were part of her process of dealing with it. She was with my grandmother sheltering her from her pain, while I tried to be there for her. I tried lightening the mood by doing things with her and telling her to see the beauty in life, not the pain and suffering we had just experienced. There were times when I needed to distance myself, going for walks, and questioning my meaning of what happens to us in the afterlife.

Death is a big part of life's experience, and often it is a part that not many of us like to discuss. My mother's afterlife beliefs were from a more logical and physical perspective that I usually didn't entirely resonate with. Sometimes I would tell her that I thought there was more to us than just this earth. It is only because of the events and experiences I have felt that have led me to my conclusions. As I am close with my mother, sometimes it would be challenging not to tune in to the negative thoughts about life that circled her mind, especially during this time.

An empath knows those who we are closer to; we feel more intensely. I held firm in my own beliefs and feelings, and this made me stronger. I took time away to be on my own when I needed to and allowed my close circle of people to be there. It meant that I could also be there for my mom without feeling like I was jeopardizing myself.

REPEATING CYCLES

Ever felt like you have been stuck in a cycle on repeat, in friendships, relationships, or work life? Round and round with no way out, like you were in a washing machine of ups and downs. Maybe you feel like you are always taken advantage of by people, or become a dumping ground for everyone's problems. Perhaps you attract the same type of toxic or abusive relationships. The truth is, if your nodding to this, you have made progress. Either you have evolved beyond these repeating patterns and have been doing the work, or know you have the issue.

Congratulations, if you have grown through it and are better for it today, breaking this pattern took me numerous years. It wasn't until I addressed all my fears about getting into another relationship and lack of self-worth that things shifted. If you know you tend to have repetitive behaviors, then you have made it past step one. Acknowledging your truths is just like turning on the light bulb.

The next steps take a little more work but are not impossible. Start with addressing what the behaviors you repeat are. You need to understand why you repeat these. I got into repetitive relationships where I wasn't respected or treated the way I wanted to be.

My need for helping others became more important than my own needs to feel loved and appreciated.

I asked myself why I felt lonely and why I was looking for a man to fulfill my need to be accepted or loved.

Taking time away from relationships to focus on me was the best thing I ever did. It took the pressure off helping others, and put it on helping and finding myself. It is what triggered a yearning for self-exploration and my understanding. Exploring my emotions, I would make it a habit to question my thoughts and feelings each time. I'd ask myself if these feelings were mine and tried to acknowledge where they derived from. I would sit in silence when I didn't have the answers and ask them to come to me. Often, they came through as a flashing image, intense feeling, or memory from my past.

My next step was to acknowledge the thoughts that came with those feelings, what was my internal dialogue playing back to myself. For example, I was not worthy or had to work very hard to see any results in life. These false beliefs then had to fall away and make room for my new ideas, the ones that aligned with me. Writing positive affirmations against my old belief system, I reprogrammed my subconscious. I built a healthier version of myself—one who was confident and self-assured in her gifts and abundance. I knew I deserved a balanced relationship where I felt like I was treated like an equal and each person took responsibility for their baggage. Until what I desired arrived, I just held tight and tried to do things that lifted me higher.

Investing in myself, I did a few short courses that pushed me to meet new people and expand out of my comfort zone. Feeling liberated and scared at the same time, it forced me to grow. On the weekends, I went to the beach and took long drives to explore new places on my own. My hair was changed to make me feel as fresh and new on the outside as I did inside.

Pushing myself, I made an effort to start dating again. Once I had built enough confidence and strength. My timing was perfect, using my intuition to tell me when I felt ready. No longer afraid of losing control in a situation, I dipped my toes into the relationship pool again, taking things super slow. After all, it wasn't a race. Even when I liked someone, I wouldn't start anything too serious until I saw what I needed to. I paid attention to the red flags without judgment. Even if I couldn't understand them completely, I acknowledged they were there. No matter how much I liked them, any guys who acted aloof or hot and cold got dismissed instantly. When someone is genuinely interested in you and mature enough for a relationship, there are no games. Typically, an empath only needs to be honest with themselves, and they will sense this.

HELPING OTHERS WITHOUT GETTING TO ATTACHED

This topic falls hand in hand with the above two cases we have just discussed. Knowing your own emotions can become more apparent once you develop a habit to discharge from the world. It would be best if you were your own disciplinary, calling yourself out.

Admit each time you feel you are being consumed or crossing over into someone's energy field. The other person may take comfort in being around you, as you help heal their wounds and leave them with a great feeling, but they can never understand what it feels like for you to be with the aftermath. My advice, spend less time with those who tend to be less giving; you know who I am talking about. Surround yourself with positive people who can appreciate your advice but also give good advice back. These beings will uplift you and make you feel more in tune with yourself.

Something I like to do is when I feel like someone negative is zapping my energy, I amplify my positive emotion by double. I envision a wall going up between me and the other, so I feel protected. I make myself aware that I am happy, healthy, and don't want this person's energy. It usually works in two ways. After each negative remark only gets thrown back with a positive comment on my end, they give in, realizing they are never going to win this battle and conform.

Or when I start to feel like nothing I say will help, I excuse myself cut it short, and walk away. Doing this doesn't mean you don't care about the person. It merely means you're not encouraging their behavior. By walking away, you allow them to process their own emotions. The more you make this a habit, the better you'll become at it.

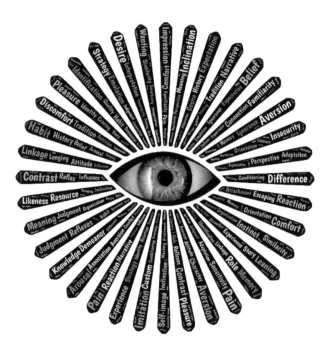

OVERCOMING GUILT

Overcoming guilt somehow comes with some of the struggles an empath faces daily. I will keep this one short and to the point. Every one of us is capable of looking out for ourselves. Just because you can feel things doesn't mean you need to feel guilty about deciding not to get involved. God gave us all free will, just like every other human on this planet, it is our decision and our consequence if we decide to do something.

If you feel guilty, remember to reassure yourself of this. Your job is not to allow yourself to be taken advantage of; it's to use what you have, to the best of your ability.

Try writing positive affirmations for yourself if you struggle with this constantly. Start by reading aloud each morning words like "It is my own choice to…" and "I am allowing feelings of guilt to pass through me, others' feelings are not my responsibility."

EVOLVING AS AN EMPATH

An empaths journey can particularly feel lonely and isolating. I struggled with years of feeling alone and misunderstood like I was the only one of my kind. But there is a reason why we have come to this world at this time. Maybe you do not know at the moment what that is. However, it will reveal itself when you are ready for it.

The soul's evolution is part of our human experience. Each of us is here to learn different lessons to grow past anything no longer serving us. For an empath, our evolvement regularly has to do with understanding our gift, self-value, and breaking repetitive cycles from past generations. The good news is that you will learn how to know yourself better and grow from your mistakes or repeating habits with time.

You may come to a point in your life where you go through a spiritual awakening, which forces you to do internal work and question your spirituality or life purpose. The truth is, there is no easy way of dealing with evolving. I would suggest talking to other like-minded souls who have been through the process of reading on the matter so you can feel relief.

An empath faces many other challenges. We know when people are lying to us and sometimes prefer to play dumb to it not to hurt the other person's feelings. But this is not okay if it affects you directly. You should feel confident in assertively expressing yourself.

Most of the time, we find it hard to say no to people and need to work on our boundaries with others. We will discuss boundaries in the next chapter, but it's good to know that you'll become better at setting boundaries with experience.

Another challenge empath's face is that we are always seeking an escape from the intense emotions we experience. This type of behavior can turn into addictive habits as a form of blocking out our feelings. I did this through traveling, each time things got too hard, and life left me feeling defeated, leaving behind my worries, I would travel abroad. It was a great way to see the world and take time out from it, allowing new experiences to unfold. But when I got back, the issues were still there.

Travel brought me the solitude and adventure I needed. It gave me time to look at aspects of my life that needed improving or didn't feel quite right. But ultimately, only by addressing things can you get past them.

Writing Task

Write down the signs & feelings you get when you need to step back and take some time. Do you feel exhausted or overwhelmed?

By understanding the emotions and patterns, you will be able to apply the action steps towards knowing when you need to step back.

Do you have any feelings you need to acknowledge or addictive behaviors? Notice why you do these; what emotions do they bring you, and why it gives you relief?

What can you do to stop these repetitive behaviors and change up your energy?

For example, if you find yourself shopping as a way of feeling better, notice why you feel like you need to have these items. Is it a way of comforting yourself or knowing you can have material wealth, or is it just receiving?

Try a different mindset like offering your time to a charity or donating stuff to someone to receive. Have a garage sale with goods you have collected that you no longer need or want. Save for a long-term goal like a trip or investment into yourself, such as learning skills in a creative course.

Follow Your North Node

"When we fail to set boundaries and hold people accountable, we feel used and mistreated" _____

Brené Brown

CHAPTER FOUR: LEARNING TO SET BOUNDARIES

I f you have ever dreaded the word 'boundaries,' you'll understand that it is because you were not aware of setting them. Boundaries are a natural part of self-respect and being human. It is caring enough about yourself and how you feel, so others do not take advantage of you.

WAYS TO SET BOUNDARIES

Empaths are incredibly compassionate towards others, and unless we learn to set clear boundaries, we can become victims of chronic fatigue.

Some of the things you can do to help set boundaries are;

o Understand we are all different. Just because you can mirror others feelings and deepest fears, it doesn't mean that people will appreciate you or your help. As we get older, we become wiser, use your intuition, and learn to assess situations so you can continue to learn to set better boundaries.

o   Block any person who makes you feel any
    form of abuse, verbal, physical, mental,
    anything! If others make you feel
    worthlessness, get angry, or attack you in any
    way, these are all warning signs to stay clear.

o   Sometimes people will not see your insights as
    gifts; these people are not for you. Don't
    waste your precious time by letting your ego
    take control over an outcome of someone
    else's situation, just because you want to fix
    that person. The only person you'll end up
    having to fix is you.

o   Please don't become a victim to someone
    else's fears or negativity; it is not yours to carry
    or encourage. Hold yourself strong. I like to
    catch this soon as I feel it; I walk away if I do
    not feel positive enough to deal with it. A
    drastic change in the environment can help.
    For example, if you are home and your parent
    or sibling's energy is interfering with your
    own, get outside, go for a walk or call a friend
    to meet up and join you.

o   Find a way of separating yourself from the
    person or situation using a logical approach,
    with statements. It takes time and practice, but
    it works. For example, create a self-talk
    dialogue. Sally feels sad. I can understand I am
    not sad. I care for Sally so I can feel what she
    feels. I choose to feel good because this is

Sally's battle to face. I will be a supportive and positive friend for Sally, and when I leave her place, so will my feelings of sadness. I trust she will overcome this as I have faith in her capabilities.

o Shift your mood right away when you feel yourself falling. Maybe by playing music, doing a meditation, or yoga.

o Don't allow the flattery or charm of another to disrupt your inner peace. Learn to read the signs of people who may be using you. You'll know because these people will never be there for you when you need them the most.

o Become aware of the feelings that are not your own, mood swings, or zaps in your good energy. Awareness is the first step to change.

o Note when people are trying to manipulate you or project their feelings onto you to control you. Educate yourself; if you know what a narcissistic person is like, you'll spot one far in advance

o Remember, it's okay to say no to things you don't want to do; others do it all the time. The people who respect these boundaries are the ones you want in your life.

o   Make time and space for yourself to refill your energy levels, spend time outside, or reading a good book. You can think more clearly when you feel energetically recharged and on top of your game.

Try and keep a balanced lifestyle of work, rest, and play. Sleep is essential, and so is taking time out when you need it. Treat yourself to a weekend away or a day trip in nature. It will keep you feeling more positive about yourself and life, while helping you to make better   decisions.

WHERE TO SET BOUNDARIES

We need to have set boundaries in many different aspects of our lives,

from our personal lives, in relationships, to our work environment.

Here are some simple tips on how to set boundaries.

At Work

Empaths generally go beyond what's expected of them; most of us dislike doing meaningless tasks or things we do not want to do. Changing jobs and careers can be quite common for an empath. If we feel taken for granted or bored, we tend to move on.

Empaths enjoy working alone or working on solo projects, as being around others can be overwhelming or distracting. Being sensitive, we require someone who can understand and meet our needs. We like to be challenged and learn and dislike office politics.

Some of the things to think about when setting boundaries at work could be;

- Please don't take on more than you can chew. It will only overwhelm you and cause stress.
- Take time out; this includes lunch breaks and small tea breaks to breathe.
- Communicate with others when you need help with something.
- Helping others with their work is fine, but only if it goes both ways, and you have already completed your tasks.
- Value your time and efforts, don't forget to ask for a pay rise and bonuses for extra work.
- Spend time unwinding from your day. Release the day's energy out by going for a walk after work or listening to some soothing music on your drive home.
- Set your intentions for the day, so you avoid procrastination and feeling overwhelmed. It will help you stay focused on the tasks you need to complete.
- It is essential for empaths to feel appreciated, make sure your boss or team knows this, and praise you for a job well done.
- Enjoy what you are working on; empaths tend to get bored easily and need to feel like they have a purpose at work. If you think you need

more stimulation or want to learn more skills, ask for growth opportunities.

At Home

Whether you are in a relationship, rental partnership, or the family environment as an empath, your home is your domain. It is a space where you probably like to spend a lot of time contemplating about life. In saying that, there needs to be boundaries set, no matter what your dynamic is.

- Respect one another's time and space. Even in a relationship, this can be more important. Empaths can quickly lose themselves in a relationship and become jumbled in the emotion of their partner, parent, or sibling.
- Make time for yourself daily, even if it is just twenty minutes a day.
- Ask for help from your flatmate or partner if you need it, with things like chores.
- Ensure your housemate is mindful of how sensitive you are to energy; this can include having unwanted strangers in the house, what you see on TV, or loud noise.
- Have a private space just for you. It may be your room or an outside courtyard area with plants.
- As an empath, you may have mothering qualities. Try not to become that role in the dynamic where you are doing everything for everyone; it needs to be balanced.

Relationships

One aspect most empaths may struggle with is relationships with others, especially deep and intimate connections. Valuing yourself in any relationship is necessary; this sets boundaries on how others treat you.

Remember these tips below;

- People will treat you how you allow them to.
- Saying no or expressing your anger, pain, or fears is part of being in a relationship.
- All relationships require an equal give and take, so you shouldn't be holding all the rope.
- Know your own space is essential, as it is your way of reconnecting with yourself.
- You do not have to be the people-pleaser, for others to like you.
- The more respect you learn to have for yourself, the better respected you will be.
- Express your needs to others without putting their needs first.
- Please do not ignore your feelings, intuition, or warning signs; address them.
- A great friendship or partnership will not feel like a struggle. It will be equally rewarding, sometimes challenging, but in the right way. When you come out the other end, you'll

both feel better connected.

TECHNIQUES TO HELP PROTECT YOU

The more awareness you have of your personal space, the better you will protect your energy. For an empath, this is a skill you will learn to develop, rather than be born with naturally.

Here is a recap on some of the things we have learned to put into practice;

- Communicate and express what you want and need from people, whether it be in friendships or relationships.
- Ask yourself is this my own emotions I am feeling. Try to question and understand why you feel a certain way, where does it stem from? It will make you catch on to your feelings more quickly when they arise.
- Create a happy space around your home and office. Include pictures of things you love that make you feel good.
- Take note when you are feeling triggered or getting drained by someone, then put it in question.

- Practice grounding techniques or meditation as a way of re-aligning with your energy and releasing any negativity.
- Spend time alone to discharge emotions, especially if you are in a relationship.
- Make sure your body is getting enough nutrition, hydration, and exercise. It will help boost those good endorphins.
- Remind yourself it's not your responsibility to take on other people's issues. Each of us is responsible for our feelings and emotions; it doesn't matter who it is. There is a difference between being a listener and dumping your negativity onto others.
- Shield yourself from strangers or negative people. I usually like to take on a persona, like I am acting. While still being compassionate. I will put up a barrier between myself and the other person to clarify that this is not my issue. You can choose a character who is confident and robust; it might be someone you already know. My character is sympathetic but dependable. You will find with time; you will become better at deflecting others. Just try it, most strangers won't even know the difference, and you'll walk away feeling lighter.
- Acknowledge some people are just born miserable or are less evolved and are comfortable being that way; therefore, it's not our job to encourage that. Tell yourself that you choose to be positive, as the situation does not benefit you by promoting their behavior.

- Talk to yourself when you are in a situation. Separate yourself from your body and emotions. Think in a very logical and rational way, rather than letting your emotions rule. Empaths can learn to block or shut emotions, in the right circumstance, you need to practice it.
- Build your self-esteem, self-worth, and confidence each day. Practice positive internal dialogue, and don't forget to praise yourself when you need to.
- Empaths should practice consistency and routine this will help to build healthy habits. It will assist you to keep a clear, logical mind.
- If you believe in something more like the spirit world, ask for guidance and support from your guides, past on loved ones, god, or whoever you believe in.
- Be mindful when sometimes we distract ourselves with other people's issues in order for us not to face our own. Learn to discover yourself, embrace who you are, your past, feelings about yourself, and be open to doing your soul's growth work.
- Practice mindfulness in simple activities to keep you feeling more in control of emotions. Baking or spending time in the garden is a great task I enjoy, where I lose my sense of time and focus just on the activity.
- Learn to separate yourself from others by not taking things personally. Not everyone is as in tune, beautifully thoughtful, and sensitive as you; otherwise, we would all be the same.

Don't get angry about it; it's just a part of human nature. Try using the experience to better connect with yourself and your inner knowing.

- Practice being the observer of the situation. Rather than taking on the other person's energy, try practicing to be detached, like an outsider watching the case play out. Give advice and listen.
- Build a network of positive people and inspiring groups of friends who motivate and understand you. Their energy will automatically raise your vibration.

THE IMPORTANCE OF DISCERNMENT & KNOWING WHAT YOU WANT

Discernment for an empath is paramount. It is your ability to judge or comprehend the details of something, to see the truth in a situation or person. Empath's natural skills can mean they can sniff out a cheat, but sometimes we tend to oversee the case for what it is.

When emotions overshadow our logical minds, it can make us vulnerable to being used or feeling disconnected from ourselves. Better still, have you ever felt like you have been in a situation where your heart or emotions were telling you one thing, while your intuition was subtly warning you of a red flag? Our feelings can be so powerful it is difficult to brush them aside; while you craved to follow your heart's desires, you know your intuition generally acts as a warning sign.

It is a crucial principle for an empath to know what they want, especially in a relationship, and not stray from this. I am not talking about the physical appearance of a person. My reference is towards what type of relationship you would like to share with another.

Does he or she need to be gentle, kind, understanding, or a good communicator? Would you like a supportive partner, someone secure, mature, culturally open?

Then look at the kind of lifestyle you would like to have, what are your interests, perhaps traveling like me, or maybe having a family is a priority.

Assess the qualities you admire, knowing what you want makes it easier to distinguish what characters you want to attract into your life. So, when a good looking, shady person comes along and doesn't have any of the qualities you desire in a person, you do not even bat an eyelid. Even if their dog just died and they have lost their job and their partner in the same week, period!

Develop base requirements and know, as an empath, you damn well deserve it.

Who else can love a person as an empath does? Know your worth, and don't ever settle for less! Even if you have an emotional bond with someone, apply more logic to the situation.

The more you do this without allowing yourself to get too attached, the healthier and happier you will become when you meet someone who has *almost* all the qualities you are looking for because, let's be realistic here, you cannot find them all.

Writing Task

Think about aspects or situations with people where you need to set better boundaries. Write down a quick action plan of the steps you will take to improve this.

For example, you feel unappreciated at work. Is this something that can change with communication, or do you need to look for another job?

If you are looking for a relationship or friendship that is equally balanced, what are the qualities you would like to attract? What kind of relationship would you like to have?

Write these all down and keep it somewhere that you can see. By focusing on it and setting your intention toward attracting better for yourself, you will see that your standards will begin to lift.

Follow Your North Node

"I care for myself. The more solitary, the more friendless, the more unsustained I am, the more I will respect myself" _____

Charlotte Brontë -Jane Eyre

CHAPTER FIVE: BEING OPEN TO CHANGE

Getting out of your comfort zone is never an easy thing, and for some people, change can be intimidating and overwhelming. When we accept change, it brings us the opportunity to expand our knowledge and experience, while resistance to change can leave us feeling stuck. There was a significant turning point, where I had to slow down and assess my life aspects. I felt so out of balance like I had fallen into a pit of negativity, further from what I desired. Dedicating so much time to my career and trying to find happiness in my life. Feeling empty and lost, I was wasting away the minutes and hours chasing my tail. If joy was a way of life, not a destination, I was doing it all wrong. I felt contradicted trying to keep realistic about the kind of lifestyle I wanted to live as I questioned a generation of manuscripts handed down. With so many changes happening in my internal and external world, these old instilled beliefs no longer made sense. If I believed I was abundant in life, I had to understand why I hadn't attracted the things I wanted most. I wanted to be in a loving relationship; my longing for an equal partner was top of my wish list and deeper meaning.

Being open to change and adjust my thoughts, took strength and courage. You may be your most significant obstacle through your beliefs about yourself and not even know it. If I never questioned my own opinions about myself that kept leading me back to the same types of relationships, nothing would have changed. There is no point carrying around the thoughts that weaken you or make you feel hopeless. By believing in these thoughts, you help to keep them alive. One technique that I learned was I would tell my unwelcomed internal negative opinion that it didn't belong. It brought me the awareness of how many negative thoughts I would receive in a day. The more I did this, the less frequent they became. I started to replace negative thinking with a positive one, and within a month, I already noticed a change in my self-confidence.

Address Your Emotions

Part of the process of change is to let your emotions flow. Don't try to suppress the things you feel because they are difficult to understand; the answers will eventually present themselves if you keep searching.

On the contrary, we don't always grow and expand when we are in a state of feeling positive or happy. Sometimes we evolve faster during times of addressing negative emotions or thoughts. These are the things that continue to present themselves to us, while the more we try to avoid them, the more they are pushed into our faces for us to address. Until you bring these things into the light and acknowledge them, the universe will continue to add them onto your path in more obvious ways.

When feelings arise, ask yourself why; if you have self-doubt, continue to ask yourself why, until you understand the deeper meaning. All the answers are there, within you, just be willing to do the work and unravel all the treasures you will find. They are treasures as they provide you with an opportunity to learn more about yourself and peel away anything that is not part of who you are. The more you know about yourself, the more you realize the connection you have between events and people in your life. Our guidance is always trying to communicate with us, even if we cannot see all the signs. Learning to trust your intuition, and developing a viewpoint outside your perspective to your situation, can shift your emotional intelligence.

When I was living on the East coast in Sydney, I became stuck in a cycle that involved spending 3 hours a day traveling to and from work. My morning commute began at 7.30 am and ended when I arrived home by 8 pm. During this period, I kept seeing the number   911.

Emotionally exhausted, I was overthinking ways to escape the life I was currently living. I knew I needed to make a drastic change, yet I wasn't sure how. Finally, giving in to my feelings, I realized that I valued quality time in my life, and I was wasting it. I decided to be open to new possibilities and shifted my vibration to welcome new growth opportunities.

Since I was single, my options were limitless just to my imagination. My soul was seeking solitude and a fresh new environment, maybe where I could be open to meeting new people and having new adventures. After traveling over to the West Coast of Australia for a short time, I realized how much I enjoyed the natural environment and space and began to apply for work in Perth. When the opportunity presented its self, four months later, I took it, embracing the change. People thought I was crazy moving to an isolated city like Perth. It was a five-hour flight from Sydney, but I felt it was what I needed. So, ignoring everyone, I did what was right for me.

The Courage to Make Changes

I had no idea how long I would stay when I first arrived in Perth. All I knew was I needed to break the busy cycle my life had become. A few years later, thanks to my openness to being vulnerable, I had learned so much about myself. My healthy daily routine became consistent, as I practiced yoga, went for walks on the beach, and read books that expanded my mind.

All my friends were in Sydney, and I only knew the people I worked with, so I had little distraction. The transition in pace to a coastal country town took some adjusting. Living in Perth was sometimes lonely, and there were times when I missed everyone. On the plus side, it provided me with a chance to embrace a new way of being. Once you are open to change and let go of resistance, you allow things to flow into your life.

These things can help guide you along the way. Being open to change and new exciting possibilities enables you to see something you wouldn't normally. When you place restrictions on yourself, you stop the natural flow of abundance.

One memorable weekend, I sat alone inside a tiny café, feeling the nearby fireplace's ambers' warmth. It was a memorably chilly day, quite unusual for Perth. I was contemplating going on a holiday and was trying to justify my reason. While waiting for my coffee, I opened my magazine to read, "As scary as it may seem, change can be exciting and open the door to new possibilities. Step through and be a master of your own moments." Simultaneously, at the same time, I hear a song playing in the background; it was a familiar tune, something I had heard years ago while traveling through Europe.

The energy I received came as a wave of nostalgia as I recalled the adrenalin rush that traveling brought me. This synchronized message that had come through was the confirmation I needed. Always enchanted by a traveler's way of life, the culture and history delighted me. Travel was in my blood, and for me, it felt more normal to live like a nomad day by day than to be stuck in a nine to five schedule. Feeling displaced between the Italian culture I grew up with and the country where I lived. I lived the Australian way; however, while in Italy, I was like a foreigner returning home after many years. I felt like a foreigner, no matter where I was.

Since finding a better life balance, I felt a holiday was just what I needed to put my awakened senses to the test. Trying not to let my limiting beliefs control me any longer, I wanted my heart to be utterly open to new abundant experiences.

Portugal

My trip begins meeting my Italian cousin Laura at the train station of Milano Centrale on platform one. After a lengthy hug, it is nice to see that not much has changed after seven years. We spend a night in Bergamo's Italian town before flying out to Porto, Portugal the following morning. Bergamo is a charming old medieval town that sat upon a steep ascending hill. Although it is already very late in the afternoon, we manage to catch the sunset and grab a bite to eat before retreating after a long travel day. By morning we arrive in Porto, and while looking for our hostel, an older man passing by offers us some help. Not speaking a word of the same language, the man passionately waves in the direction that we need to go, expressing himself in Portuguese before practically walking us to our hostel.

Porto is a beautiful city with pastel-colored houses, all detailed with elegantly crafted tiles and orange terracotta rooftops. Succumbing to the tourist trap, we enjoy a coffee at the famous Majestic café. The cafe is full of people spilling out from the restaurant onto the busy main street. Later that day, we cruise the

Douro River under its six bridges, eat bacalhau, a famous dried fish dish, and sample the Duoro Valley wines.

Visiting the beautiful bookstore Lello & Irmão felt like a Harry Potter movie scene, with its spiraling staircase, red carpet, and ambient yellow lighting. And rumor has it that the author's inspiration came from this bookstore after living in Porto. For me, it had to be one of the most beautiful bookstores in the world, with its neo-gothic façade and interior wooden walls and stain glass ceiling. After three days in Porto, we make our way to Aveiro by train for one night. Aveiro is known as the mini Venice, mini indeed. Less touristy and very quaint with its Art Deco buildings, gondolas, and striped houses lined up along the lagoon.

Sitting in an outdoor restaurant that evening, we found ourselves entertained by our waiter, who provided many giggles. He would scoot around from table to table, in and out of the kitchen like re-run scenes from John Cleese's 1970s Faulty Towers.

Sintra's next stop quickly became one of my favorite towns, and it is difficult not to succumb to its grander, from the picturesque palaces and castles to the stunning mountains. Arriving at our lovely hostel, we leave our bags to find a little cafe not too far from the station. We order our morning tea of coffee, and homemade orange cake. Once it arrives, we marvel at the generous portion size; one piece of cake could feed the two of us. Between us, we had half a cake; lucky we are hungry and polish our plates clean. Afterward, we hop on the local bus that takes us to Pena Castle, one of the many castles. The bus was crammed with tourists with hardly any air to breathe, winding up the winding and narrow road with passengers swaying side to side. We were amazed at how these drivers take control of a large vehicle on such tight roads. Reaching our first glimpse of the castle, we see how truly astonishing it is. Just like something out of a Disney fairytale, Pena castle is 19th century Romanticism at its finest. The court features Moorish period detailing and a beautiful tonal palette, with its interior equally fascinating. We spend half the day exploring its many rooms and admire the view as it crowns the mountain overlooking Sintra's city. Very cold when the sun goes down, it sits above a rocky peak of 480 meters and is the second-highest viewpoint. Exiting the castle, we make our way back to the bus stop, passing a park with many tall pine trees. Out in the open is a photographic exhibition; I notice the year's travel photographer exhibit set among the lush green surroundings. The universe lights me up once again with experiences like this, and we spend a few moments taking in the emotions that the images evoke. Two nights later, we bid farewell to Sintra and make our way to the capital Lisbon.

Looking forward to Lisbon, I found it so well preserved and cleaner than I imagined for Europe's oldest capital cities. After almost 2700 years, the city radiates vibrant color and beauty. We are limited to just two nights, so we walk non-stop to see all the sights. Discovering Belem tower, which honors the world's famous explorers, we also take a ride on the old tram number 28 as it rattles and narrowly curves around the old city walls. The tram passes all the tourist districts, stopping at St George's castle, we hop out for the beautiful view overlooking the city. Lisbon has many hills, seven to be exact, with each one telling its own story. Taking in the sights, I admire the beautiful terracotta rooftops and whitewashed houses overlooking the blue ocean. Our apartment was centrally located right near a train station with cafes below interrupting our morning sleep-in. We watched the systematic chaos unfold from our balcony as carts, trucks, and vendors yell out, bringing food and supplies to the many local restaurants. The last evening in Lisbon, we visit Barrio Alto, which translates to the upper district. This part of town came alive in the evening when the narrow streets are full of many eateries and people dining outside. Fado music could be heard in the background as the streets came alive in complete celebration. Fairy lights and hanging colored streamers brought a party-like atmosphere to these narrow laneways, where celebrating life felt like an evening ritual. Time in Portugal was flying as we said farewell to this country after ten amazing days. My cousin and I part ways until we meet again in Italy. Portugal provided a fantastic cultural experience; its unique energy, richly preserved history, and beautiful natural countryside filled me with a desire to return and explore its many hidden gems.

Observation Task

Each time I allowed myself to be vulnerable and open to change, I welcomed new growth and possibility. Recalling how frightened I was in my twenties I had no idea what to expect during my first time alone overseas. On the other side of the world, with no phone GPS to get around, just guidebooks and maps, the experience taught me to trust myself. Once I was open to applying a change in situations, mostly where I was scared, it just seemed to elevate me on my path towards   growth.

Fear almost always gets in the way of change, and the more we can listen to why we are afraid, the more we can learn to overcome it through trusting in ourselves and our intuition.

Know that whatever you are going through, it's essential to address your fear when it comes up. Think of a time when you were so scared to trust yourself or put yourself out of your comfort zone to find that the experience brought about growth and empowerment. Try applying these steps next time something comes up. Listen to your emotions and allow yourself to feel things.

When something negative arises, try to replace it with a positive thought instead. Take note of the messages within yourself and around you, and don't be afraid to act on them. Being open to change can help us to flourish in ways we never imagined for ourselves.

CHAPTER SIX: ACCEPTING RESPONSIBILITY FOR YOUR MANIFESTATIONS

Every one of us vibrates with energy, whether we are aware of it or not. We are continuously transmitting a signal, regardless of if we are in a good or bad mood. Sometimes we can pick up on the emotions of one another even before being communicated. Through body language, tone, and energy, we can feel the vibration of one another. It is more evident when we know the person, be it a partner, child, or close friend, as their energy is familiar to us.

Have you ever noticed when you are in a perfect mood, how things seem to line up for you? When we are in the flow of life and feel good, we emit good positive vibes outwards, which attracts positivity back to us. It is known as the law of attraction, which can be useful in many different aspects of our lives.

What You Believe You Attract

Manifesting becomes more comfortable when you have a good relationship with yourself, learning to accept responsibility for our actions, feelings, and manifestations. We display things every day, sometimes without even knowing. It is difficult to digest when things don't play out the way we had imagined or envisioned for ourselves. Sometimes this is due to our contradictory beliefs or behaviors. These contradictions can push us away from what we want and are usually signs that we need to do more work to release false blockages.

By focusing on what you want, while applying healthy action, you can manifest your desires. As like attracts like, if you're going to attract the perfect partner or job to your life, then you need to become that ideal vibrational match.

The reason why I felt ready to have a relationship was different than why I hadn't attracted the right partner into my life. Of course, I wanted to have a caring and equally balanced partnership. But if I didn't believe I was deserving of it or put the other person's needs before my own, I would never attract the right person. It wasn't until I decided to focus on myself and my worth that I attracted an abundance of people, both in my friendships and relationships, that appreciated me for who I was. They saw the value in me because I finally treated myself in a way where I valued who I was.

Acknowledging my potential and unique qualities, I set boundaries with how I treated myself and, in turn, others picked up on these vibrations. The negative feelings went away, and I could express myself confidently in a caring yet powerful way.

I remember there was a point in my trip overseas when I was traveling where I felt lonely. My thoughts wandered as I said out loud to the universe that I wanted to have the opportunity to make great friendships while I was away. Little did I know I had planted the seed, and immediately my prayers were being answered, flourishing the following day naturally.

Manifesting Effortlessly

Florence, Italy

After arriving by plane from Geneva, I wait for my bags at Florence airport's baggage claim area. This beautiful French woman swiftly brushes past me, reaching for her bright yellow suitcase before it went around the conveyor belt for the second time. Stepping out of her way, she throws me a smile while looking over her shoulder. Giggling and murmuring something in French, she rolls her suitcase towards the exit.

Once I get a hold of my bag, I head over to the bus stop that goes to Florence's central train station, as I am on my way to stay with my cousin Laura. I see the same French woman sitting pretty in her navy blue and tiny white floral printed dress at the bus stop. She is tall and slim, carrying a cute blunt bob hairstyle. Her lap is a small straw brimmed hat with a red ribbon, the kind only French women wear. Turning to her, I ask if the bus goes to the train station and it all started from there. We sat next to each other on the bus and chatted the whole way. I discovered her name was Nat; she lived in France and was on holiday visiting Florence for a few days. We laugh and say it is destiny to meet when we find out that she sat directly in front of me on the plane.

When the bus reached the station half hour later, the other passengers exited the backdoor while we continued chatting. The last one to leave the bus, we stand outside the station with our suitcases about to say goodbye when Nat mentions it's a shame that I will not be staying. Realizing that I felt the same way, I quickly thought about why I shouldn't stay in Florence for the night. After all, I was traveling, and the adventure was entirely in tune with my manifestation of wanting to make genuine friendships.

My spontaneous decision to see if I could get a room for the night at the same hotel as Nat made us laugh with excitement. Still talking, we drag our suitcase over the bumpy cobblestones and turn down the bendy streets till we reached an open piazza. We were entering the beautifully decorated hotel, which had an old renaissance style, and found a room. After check-in, we walk through the hotel lounge to see a little courtyard with a magical view overlooking this enchanting city. Once I connected to the hotel internet, I send a message to my cousin telling her I would arrive the following day.

It's a warm summer's afternoon; we wander through narrow streets and stumble across another square containing multiple cafes. Sitting under a shaded umbrella, we order a pizza to share. There is such an energetic connection, as we continue to chat about our lives, nothing feels uncomfortable. The more I speak to her, the more it feels like we are old friends from another time. We spend just over an hour digesting before deciding to sample the best gelato in Florence. When we reach the place, the line is almost out the door, but we manage to squeeze inside the air-conditioned shop. The smell of chocolate and waffles penetrates the air as the line shuffles forward, bringing us a little closer to the counter. Most gelato enthusiast's eyes would pop at the overwhelming choice of flavors on offer; they had every flavor imaginable.

While others continued to line up behind us, we finally reach the front of the line. We make our selections, pay, and pick up shuffling past customers trying to enter the store as we exit. With our gelato in hand, we walk along the Arno River. The buildings, architecture, and walkways all have a story to tell, and I understand why so many creatives want to call this place home. You can feel the energy from famous artists whose spirit still lingered amongst the hidden laneways and many bridges. As I take a deep breath, I try to absorb it all and feel nothing but happiness. My senses came alive; I had gelato for my taste buds, a beautiful city to marvel over, with buskers playing music for my ears. What more I could ask. We spend the afternoon watching the sunset over the terracotta rooftops from our hotel balcony. The sleepy sky goes from a bright beaming yellow to a magnificent streak of orange across the hazy Florentine sky. As the bonging sound of multiple church bells echoes in the distance, it feels like we are in a place from another time.

Back in the room, we play music while getting ready for dinner, located just a few streets away. Walking into the restaurant, we were greeted by the smell of truffle oil and seated nearby a window overlooking the dimly lit laneway. The place is modern and cozy with its timber setting and red and white checked tablecloth. Homemade bread with a cream cheese spread gets dropped off to our table before the waitress takes our order. The timber beams and warm color palette make it feel like we are dining as guests at someone's home. When our delicious plates of homemade pasta arrive, it looked and smelt amazing! Sampling one another's choices, we toast to our meeting with a glass of Tuscan wine.

Taking our time to eat, we savor each mouthful, enjoying the flavor. We decide to stretch our insides with dessert and order a baked cheesecake. Dessert arrives showered in strawberry coulis and a mountain of fresh berries. Another generous portion, and by the second spoonful, my belly had urged me to stop. Hours passed until we were one of the last ones left in the restaurant. Trying to digest, we took to the street for a long walk. The roads dotted with people walking and window shopping; most of the buskers had finished for the night. The city seemed sleepy, so we decided to retreat to our hotel to conserve our energy for the following day.

After breakfast the next morning, Nat walks me to the train station as I make my way north to visit my cousin. Promising to keep in touch, we make a rough plan to meet up again before the European summer ends. While searching for my wallet to pay for my train ticket, I feel Nat drop something into my open bag. The day before I complimented her on her taste in jewelry, I look inside my handbag and pull out one of her silver bangles. "Ah no," I drag out in disbelief. She pleads with me, saying she wants me to keep it as a memory of our meeting and friendship. Lost for words, and overcome with a mix of emotions. Destined to meet Nat in Florence, maybe fate would have it that we would become great friends. We give each other a big hug and look back to watch the other walk away.

Observation Task

Manifesting comes with ease once you learn to allow your path to unfold, without holding onto too much of the 'how' it will happen. Once you develop momentum in your vibration, then that's when you can start to see the results. Try and play with manifestation and test your skills; too many of us take life too seriously. Start small by changing the routine in your mornings to create more positive vibes throughout your day. Meet a friend for coffee before work or have a chat with someone you haven't called in a long time to see how they are going. By changing up your vibes in a positive way, it can increase your chances of attracting better things into your day. Set a positive intention and see if you can allow the outcome to play out the way you envision it. Tools you can use to manifest your desires are positive affirmations. These are words you can write yourself to help you believe in your desired outcome. A positive affirmation could be something you want to occur in your life or words about yourself to uplift and inspire you. When I write my assertions, I try and keep them realistic and honest for myself and change them as I become more confident and closer to my goal. For example, an affirmation could be, "I am trusting in my capabilities to find my life path." Or "I am blessed with abundance, so it is safe for me to explore my options." By writing and reading your affirmations daily, I guarantee after a few weeks, once you pass the stage of uncomfortable, your confidence will start to change. It is something that initially I felt very unsure of as the relationship with myself was so disconnected. Saying these out loud is more powerful as it is you affirming your belief to yourself. I noticed a change in my attitude towards myself; the more I persevered past the emotions of feeling like a fraud, I started to believe in what I was reading and saying aloud. With patience and practice, you will too. Having a clear goal will help you stay focused and driven.

AUTHORS MESSAGE

Through good and bad, I try to embrace life to focus on my inner world. I hope is that you feel inspired to believe in yourself and follow your destined journey to happiness. If you'd like to read more of my work or get in touch, I also write for a website called Planet Intuition and would love to continue this journey of growth and expansion with you.

Best wishes.

Good luck.

CPSIA information can be obtained
at www.ICGtesting.com
Printed in the USA
BVHW070355230221
600781BV00007B/1264